TRUTH
ABOUT
CHURCH
WOUNDS

TRUTH
ABOUT
CHURCH
WOUNDS

part of the God-Help Series

Pamela Mertz

Table of Contents

Preface

When I got the idea to write this Study, it was because I was in the midst of my own recovery from yet another wound from the hand of "church" people, even leaders, and I needed to know more about God's plan for me as I was healing. I was angry, and hurt, and wrestling with God about "His church" and what the heck?!? I was so tired of the human component of church, I even contemplated not ever again going to a building for church. I had been so wounded and spiritually abused, I was
DONE.

Then God began to stir something in me. I wasn't the only one that had these hurts and had either left "organized religion" or was feeling similar feelings that I was sharing. I told a few people I trusted about this idea God gave me to study this topic and create a Bible Study and received great support. I even was able to pull together a Test Group to go through the Study itself and they were amazing at giving me some feedback. I am very grateful to them all! Karen, Patty, Britney, Robin, Kelsey, and others. Thank you for sharing your time, your hurts, and your hearts with me so that I could polish this up and create something that God wants out there for His people.

I am betting that as you read this, there is lots stirring within you too, dear friend. You have been searching to better understand the "why" of the wounds you have experienced. Perhaps you have been recently wounded and are still reeling back on your heels in shock; or maybe you have stuffed the pain for years and are simply tired of the continual gnawing that is always in the background of your days. Whatever happened to you that resulted in a wound at church, please know that I have been praying for you, and most of all, know that God wants to heal this too. He is after us and pursues us to be able to do all that He wants to do in our lives. When we stop and rest, letting Him provide that healing, it happens.

You have this in your hand for a reason. You have been wounded or know someone who has been wounded by church. You are searching for answers, some rational explanation about "why", or even if church is even still for you. My hope is that you will find what you are searching for during this Study. I trust that you are gathered with a group of people that you feel safe with and you will be able to share your "church wound" experience. In doing so, I pray that you, the reader and participant in this Study, will be able to receive some healing from God as He leads you through this time of clarity and deeper understanding of the hurts you have and into a fresh new awareness of purpose in the healing process.

Blessings and Healing, my friends.

Introduction

How To Use This Study

This Study is designed to be used by a small group, using the Bible to interpret itself and seeking to learn from original texts of Hebrew and Greek languages, by using a Strong's Concordance.

You will need a facilitator or leader, as well as your Bibles to participate fully in the Study. If anyone has a Strong's Concordance, NASB version, that would be helpful to have as well.

As a leader, please pray about who to invite into this study and know that church wounds vary in severity and depth. We are not going to compare wounding but seek the needed healing in this time together.

How To Use a Strong's Concordance

The following are instructions of how to use a Strong's Concordance from www.gotquestions.org :

Why use a concordance?

- A concordance is a helpful tool when doing a word study. Using an exhaustive concordance, you can locate every occurrence of the word in the Bible and gain helpful insight into what it means.
- A concordance is helpful in learning the definitions of Greek, Hebrew, or Aramaic words.
- A concordance is helpful when trying to locate a Bible verse, when unable to remember the chapter and verse.

How does a Bible concordance work? Perhaps you remember a verse about Noah finding grace in the eyes of the Lord, but you can't remember where it is found. You can look up grace in a concordance in order to discover the reference. Here is an excerpt from the entry for grace:

GRACE

Genesis 6:8, But Noah found g. in the eyes of the... H2580
Genesis 19:19, Behold now, thy servant hath found g... H2580
Genesis 32:5, my lord, that I may find g. in thy sight... H2580

You notice the verse you're looking for is Genesis 6:8, the one that mentions Noah. While you're at it, you can look up other instances of the same Hebrew word translated "grace." Notice that Genesis 19:19 and Genesis 32:5 have the same reference number in the right column. Those two verses use the same Hebrew word (numbered H2580).

Then you can look up the definition of the Hebrew word translated "grace" by using the reference number. At the back of the concordance, you will find this entry for H2580:

"H2580 chēn from H2603 chanan; graciousness, i.e. Subjective (kindness, favor) or Objective (beauty): — favour, grace(-ious), pleasant, precious, (well-)favoured."

A Bible concordance, whether online or in print, is a valuable resource for any student of the Bible. It is a basic tool and is often one of the most used in Bible study.

Now let's dive in!

Group leader, open in prayer.

Code of Confidentiality

This study is designed to help heal and not bring more hurt.

As a member of this small group, I agree to keep all things said in this group in confidence and will not speak of it outside of this group without express consent from that person.

This is a safe place to share, and I want to operate in a culture of honor.

I will not compare church wounds – or negate in any way – the healing process of another.

Signature _____

Date _____

What Is Church?

Defining the Church – What does the Bible say?

F or generations, we have heard about "going to church" and that the "church building" is where church is and church work happens. To best define the church, it is important to look at what the Bible actually says about how to define what Church is. I have been on a journey myself to understand the church. I love the Church and church people. However, there have been many people that have been hurt by the very people that they long to trust and have relationship with.

As a little girl, I loved going to Sunday School, and my Sunday School teachers, especially Jenny, were so loving and delighted in me. I felt safe and loved. When we moved across country when I was age 12, we went to a small-town church (town was 89 people!). It was there in Pioneer Girls that I was introduced to Jesus and prayed the prayer of repentance and salvation at age thirteen. My pal, May, was the sweetest, most gentle woman I had encountered, and that tiny pilot light within me instantly shot up on size and strength. I felt something change within me, and I knew something had happened that was a big deal! I wanted more of that and began searching, learning, and growing. As with us all, it is a journey that begins with a small step of faith.

This study is for you to best determine how to view the Church with clarity, using only the Bible as a reference. That is, after all, the Word of

Truth. Let's dive into this discovery together and see what God wants us to know about church.

Old Testament Church

There are many terms used in the Old Testament about the gathering of God's people. The most used are two terms, *congregation* and *assembly*, which we will explore in greater detail, allowing God's Word to interpret itself.

    1. Congregation (H5712-eda, feminine noun) – defined as a gathering.

        • As a group, read Exodus 12 out loud, dividing up verses.

        • What is the context of this first mention of congregation?

        • What is God establishing in this historic event?

        • What does this mean to you as a Follower of Jesus? Discuss.

    2. Assembly (H6951-qahel, masculine noun) – defined as an organized body with purpose.

        • Read Leviticus 4:13-21 out loud.

- What is being communicated here in these verses about "church" life? Discuss.

  Deeper thoughts about these terms for discussion:

  Notice how congregation (H5712 eda – feminine noun) and assembly (H6951 – qahel – masculine noun) are used. In what context are these words used?

  We are to come to the assembly, confess, and be cleansed of sin (which is a foreshadowing of the "one anothering" of New Testament living).

- We need our congregation to help us with the mistakes we make that invite sin in. This was established in the Old Testament! *(Jesus clarified it and perfected it, making a way for us as He is the Way.)*

- What is happening for you as you ponder these Biblical concepts? Discuss.

  Let's take a look at two more terms:

  3. Tabernacle – defined as church tent, being Holy.

- Read Exodus 30:26-29 (Moses instructed)

- Read Leviticus 8:10 (Moses doing as instructed)

- Read Numbers 7:1 (Moses recorded historically as doing as Lord said)

4. Sanctuary – we are God's sanctuary – wow! Read Psalm 150 out loud as a group and let that sink in. Right now, in this group, in your midst, the Creator Himself has taken up sanctuary. Let that soak in.

New Testament Church

Theologians refer to something called the "Law of First Mention". It means that the first mention of anything in the Bible, as a general rule, reveals significant facts to us and are consistent throughout Scripture. The subject is then studied throughout Scripture to gain further knowledge and understanding of the concepts God is trying to communicate. It's really important to look deeply at every first mention, including context, so that we can understand more of what God wants us to know about the concept.

The first mention of church in the New Testament is in Matthew 16.

The word "church" is *ekklesia* (in Greek) and means to be "taken out of" – separated from the world – in other words, *holy*.

Read Matthew 16:18 out loud.

1. Who builds the church?

2. This Rock is also referenced in Matthew 7:25, Romans 9:33 (references Isaiah 8:14), Genesis 49:24, 1 Corinthians 10:4 (look these up and read them out loud).

3. If Jesus builds the church, what role are we to play in church growth in our own churches?

   • What does that look like?

   • How has this truth been misinterpreted?

   • How do we provide those around us with this wisdom?

Conflict Happens in the Church, Too!

Conflict happens, especially in churches, and Jesus knows that. (We will learn more about this in Session Four – Warfare.) He provided us with a clear outline of conflict resolution *IN THE CHURCH.*

Have someone read Matthew 18:15-20 out loud.

   • What is this telling us about the church?

- Discuss how you have used this with examples of outcomes and discuss what happens when this model is not used.

- What are the pitfalls of unresolved conflict?

- Discuss the "two or three are gathered in My Name". What is the context of this Scripture and how do we apply this in our daily life?

See how this was done in Acts 15 in the record of the Council of Jerusalem as well. Witnesses are a part of church life (more on this in Session Five – One Anothers).

Church as Defined in Some New Testament Verses

Read these out loud and record what we learn about the Church.

1. Acts 2:46-47

2. 1 Corinthians 11:18-34

3. Matthew 5:13

4. Ephesians 5:25-27

5. Acts 12:5

6. Acts 20:28

7. 1 Corinthians 14:12

8. Ephesians 5:24

9. Ephesians 5:28-32

10. Revelation 2:1, 8, 12, 18 & 3:1, 7, 14

11. Revelation 19:7

My Role in the Church

This is for individual study to learn more about what the Bible says about our roles.

1. *Who* am *I* in the Church as a "member of the body"? (1 Corinthians 12:12-27, Ephesians 3:15)

2. Does anyone have a more important part in the body? What does this look like compared to how we view church? (We will look at this more in Session Two.)

3. Where does God dwell in the New Covenant? (Ephesians 2:21, 3:17; 1 Corinthians 3:16-17; 1 Corinthians 6:19)

4. How do I live this truth out in the Body? In my daily life?

What Does It Mean to Be "in Christ"?

For deeper study, you can look up in your Strong's Concordance or on blueletterbible.com "in Christ" to learn all that we RECEIVE in Christ Jesus. As a challenge, do a study on that, as well as look further into verses with "in Him", "as a brethren", and even using the "body" to search for more of what the Church gets to have lavished upon us because we are "IN CHRIST". (See Appendix A for a list of all "in Christ" verses to get you started.) Here are just a couple to read and discuss:

1. "A New Creation in Christ" – 2 Corinthians 5:17

    - How is this defined by God's Word?

2. "Ministry given" – 2 Corinthians 5:18

    - What is this ministry?

    - How is it defined?

    - How do I live this out in my life?

    - How will I change my thought life in my daily activities?

Ministry of Reconciliation

Reconciliation is shown in the above verses as reconciliation to God first, and then with others. As a believer in Christ, and a part of His Church, this is the only ministry assigned by God. Let that sink in. You can choose to walk more fully in that as God leads.

In Romans 5:11, reconciliation is defined as "we received the blessing of the recovered favor of God".

I accept and acknowledge that I am a Minister in God's Church – a Minister of Reconciliation.

I, _____, am a Minister of Reconciliation. I choose to walk in that manner beginning today, as God leads.

Signed _____

Date _____

More Terms to Define Church

Many other terms for the Church, as we now define it, are used in the Old Testament and New Testament. God says a lot about His Church – He must want us to know about it!

Each term and the number of times it was used throughout Scripture are listed below. Look up each of the references and note what you observe about each of them.

1. House of Prayer (4x) – Isaiah 56:7; Matthew 21:13

2. House of God (78x) – Joshua 9:23; Matthew 12:4; 1 Timothy 3:15; Hebrews 10:21

3. Sanctuary (150x) – Exodus 25:8; Isaiah 8:14; Nehemiah 10:39; Daniel 8:11, 13-14; Hebrews 8:2, 9:1-2

4. Tabernacle (128x) – Exodus 26:11; Psalms 15:1; Hebrews 8:2, 5, 9:2, 11; Revelation 13:6, 21:3

5. Temple (258x) – 1 Samuel 1:9; Ezra 4:1; Matthew 4:5; Luke 18:10

6. Zion (162x) – Psalms 9:11; Isaiah 35:10; Jeremiah 31:6, 50:5; Joel 1:1,15

7. Holy Place (76x) – Exodus 28:28; Joshua 5:15; 1 Kings 8:8; Matthew 24:5; Acts 6:13, 21; Hebrews 9:12-25

8. Holy Temple (16x) – Psalms 5:7; Jonah 2:4,7; Habakkuk 2:20; Ephesians 2:21, 3:17; 1 Corinthians 3:17

9. My Father's House (19x) – John 2:16, 14:2

Wrap Up Questions

1. We covered a lot of ground in this first Session. What is your one take away from this time together?

2. What is one thing you will do differently as a result of this time in God's Word?

3. Look ahead at the Prework for next time we meet. There are some Bible verses to look up to come prepared for discussion.

Additional Notes:

Additional Study

List some things of what you believe about the purpose of the Church below:

Next, look up the following Scriptures and write what you learn about the purpose of the Church. Are there some similarities in your pre-conceived beliefs about the Church?

Verse	What did you learn about the purpose of the Church?
Hebrews 2:12	
1 Corinthians 12:1-14:33	
2 Corinthians 5:17-20	
Ephesians 3:10	
Matthew 28:18-20	
1 Corinthians 12:7	
1 Thessalonians 5:11	
Hebrews 10:25	
1 Peter 2:4-5	
Romans 12:1	
James 5:14	
Acts 2:42	
Colossians 1:18	
2 Timothy 4:2-3	
1 Timothy 2:1-6	
Mark 16:15-20	
Ephesians 4:16	
Hebrews 4:3	
Ephesians 5:21	
Galatians 5:16-26	
Matthew 5:10-12	
1 Corinthians 12:28	

SESSION TWO

Purpose of the Church

The Purpose of the Church – What do we *do*?

As a child, I believed the purpose of the church was to help out people when they needed it, provide funerals and weddings for people in the church and community, and be a place of refuge for people that need to know the love of God. I saw this played out quite bit as a teen, as well as in my adult church experiences. I experienced funeral luncheons that were put on by the church ladies; I saw church members help out with plowing or mowing for those shut in or in need of some help. I also experienced such a great outpouring of love as a mother when my oldest son was killed in a car accident. The church surrounded us and brought meals for over a month and volunteered using donated materials and labor to build us the back deck on our house, so we would feel "held", and continued to minister to us for years afterward by checking in on us. The church also helped us create a memorial garden and gave us trees to memorialize Jeremy's life as ongoing. This was the church in action and doing life "on purpose" to love us well when we were in most need of consolation and comfort.

However, there are other things that happen in churches; this is where much wounding can come in. Leaders can become overzealous and controlling, demanding that they are the only authority in members' lives, gossip can create deep wounds in a matter of seconds, and abandonment at the time of need can be wounding by not attending to members' needs.

Well-meaning leaders can judge harshly and leave a deep wound as a result. I experienced this when my childhood pastor refused to perform my wedding ceremony because I was expecting a baby. His actions created more shame in my already difficult situation. It was less than loving. I have forgiven him, but it took years for that wound to heal and to not feel "less than".

While we all have our own ideas of the purpose of the church, based on our own experience, let us look at what the Bible says about church and what it is designed to do and be.

Group Discussion Points

- What did you discover about the Church's purpose in the verses you looked up (page 13)?

- What were you familiar with and what was a new revelation?

Edifying and Equipping the Saints seems to be a big task for the Church. Read Ephesians 4 out loud and discuss what you learn about what this means and how we live this out personally.

- What does it mean to edify the saints?

- What does it mean to equip the saints?

Group Discussion Points

In this study, we will briefly touch on the gifts given to the Church, In 1 Cor 12, these gifts are of the Spirit; in Ephesians 4, these are given by Jesus; and the final component of the Trinity is the Father. In Romans 12, He gives us our redemptive, or motivational gifts. These seven gifts are who we are, and we use these as nouns in our lives, and the other gifts are verbs/actions of how we walk out our purposes to "be" the Church to one another and to the world. This is another big topic, that you may want to research on your own to learn more about all the gifts, from whom they came to the Church, and how they operate together for one purpose: to bring glory to the Father.

Briefly review Romans 12:1-8 aloud as a group, or have just one read. Listen for context, that God has allotted to each a measure of faith, for the Body, and then the gifts that differ.....

What stands out to each of you as you truly listen to Rom 12 passage?

Read 1 Corinthians 12:28 out loud and then discuss the roles of each gift of the Spirit. What do each look like in today's Church?

What is the *order* of these ministries? Look again at 1 Cor 12:28. Is this how the church looks today? Let's use the Strong's to learn about the original definition intended in the Bible.

1. First: Apostles

   Strong's: G652, *apostolos* – one who is sent, messenger sent for with orders with great power

2. Second: Prophets

   Strong's: G4396, *prophetes* – one through whom God speaks; revealer, foreteller, divinely inspired

3. Third: Teachers

   Strong's: G1320, *didaskalos* – teacher, master, one who by great power as teachers draws crowds

4. Fourth: Miracles

   Strong's: G1411, *dynamis* – power and might, strength, moral power and excellence of soul

5. Fifth: Gifts of Healing
   Strong's: G2386, *iama* – healing

   Let's look again at 1 Corinthians 12:28: "...appointed in the church, first apostles, second prophets, third teachers..."

6. Then: Helps

   Strongs: G484, *antelempsis* – help, support, take hold of (used only this one time)

7. Then: Administration
   Strongs: G2941, *kybernesis* – government, directorship

8. Then: Various Kinds of Tongues
   Strong's: G1100, *glossa* – tongue or language

   Eph 4:1-13

9. Next: Evangelists
   Strong's: G2099, *euangelistēs* – a preacher of the gospel

10. Next: Pastors
    Strong's: G4166, *poimen* – shepherd; to care for a flock

Illustration of 5 Gifts of Jesus, with Jesus as the Cornerstone

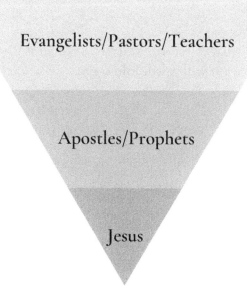

How the Gifts Are Used in the Church

Gifts of the Father from Romans 12:3-8 are often referred to as motivational gifts, or redemptive gifts. This is how you were designed and this gift, given by the Father according to the measure of faith, is what energizes you to do for the Body. Other facets of other gifts may work together with these core gifts, but this is truly how you operate in your life, by His design. (See Redemptive Gift test in Appendix C)

Ephesians 2:20 tells us that apostles and prophets lay the foundation, being built upon Jesus Christ the cornerstone. We then are living stones (1 Peter 2:5). Let's look at what Peter and Paul tell us about *how* we live this out in our daily lives:

1. Serve One Another (Gal. 5:13) - Through love, to serve one another and the world (Gal 5:13) How can you serve others? Ask the Lord to reveal your place He has for you.

2. The BODY – What part am I? (1 Corinthians 12:14-27)
   If you don't know what your spiritual gifts are, see Appendix C for some links to take a spiritual gifts test.

3. Churches that operate well with functioning parts (read Ephesians 4:16) will fulfill John 14:12.

   • Have you seen this in churches? What have you seen/experienced?

4. Go and tell the world the Gospel: The Great Commission. (Matthew 28:18-20)

   • Where are you called to carry the gospel? We all have circles of influence in each of these areas. Jot down names of people you know in each of these categories:

   Jerusalem - Your friends, family, neighbors

   Samaria – Your city

   Judea – Your region or state

   The ends of the earth – Where else you can have impact in the rest of the world

5. Walk as you were called. (1 Corinthians 7:17)

- This means to be present in your circumstances: not to desire lofty positions in the church, or to negate or neglect a leadership role, but to be who God created you to be now with Christ in you. Set apart, holy, and part of the Body, that is Christ. How does this look for you personally?

- Look at examples in Bible. How did Paul use his life as Saul? He was zealous and a teacher. Those character qualities were used in the redeemed Paul, too. What about John? Beloved, relationship-minded; it looked different than we would have thought as his life played out in exile. However, this relationship desire allowed John to be used in such intimate ways to write the Revelation of Jesus Christ!

6. How to behave in the Church. (1 Timothy 3:15; read all of 1 Timothy to get context of this behavior)

7. Glorify God – to make known the manifold wisdom of God in the heavenlies. (Ephesians 3:10)

- What does this look like? Did you realize you, as a part of the Church, have a role in making God's wisdom known to the spiritual realm? We have been given an assignment to make it known, spiritually, the manifold (Strong's: G4182, polypoikilo – which means much variegated, multi-colored) wisdom of God to whom? How do we do this? How are you doing that in your life as a part of the Church?

8. Avoid contrary doctrine. (Romans 16:17)

    - Discuss what this means. How do we know contrary doctrine? Those in retail are taught how to quickly identify a counterfeit $20 bill. They do this by studying the real thing.
    - We can apply that to the Bible. Study it, read it, know it, so that when a contrary or false teaching comes across our radar, we can quickly identify it! (Remember, in retail, clerks are taught to study the real currency, so as to be able to recognize the counterfeit.)

Wrap Up Questions

1. In light of what you learned in Session Two, who is entrusted with these tasks of the Church? Pastors only? Deacons/overseers? What about leaders?

2. Warfare: Have you struggled with your gifting and calling? Has this been an area of wounding for you at all? Why do you think this is? Share a bit of this journey with the group. (We will go more deeply into this topic in Session Four.)

3. Read some of the "in Christ" verses out loud as a group (located in the appendix). What are some that are especially stirring for you? Discuss why.

4. How will you be different in/at church, AS the Church after this session's lesson?

5. What is your biggest "aha" this week? Write it down.

Additional Notes:

Church History

Looking Back – Where Have We Come From and How Did We Get Here?

I have studied church history in depth multiple times and it is always fascinating! There is so much that has happened that has shaped the church today, with all of the denominations, and different ways of being a part of a church.

My early church experience was in Christian Science, which I now understand to be a cult. I then moved into a Baptist- leaning nondenominational church and learned about Jesus. I then joined a United Methodist Church as a young mom, bringing my young boys to Sunday School, and beginning my first Bible Study and having my oldest son confirmed. After being remarried and moving, we joined a Lutheran Church where my middle son went through confirmation and we weathered the ELCA split. There was much controversy during that time.

We now belong to a Baptist church where our mission statement is to "Love God, Love Others, and Make a Difference". It's based on the *Simple Church* model by Thom S. Rainer. The Great Commandments and Great Commission rolled into one statement of purpose.

Have you ever stopped to think about how all of the denominational differences might look to someone who has never heard the Gospel, nor grown up around "church life" as we may have known it? It would seem very confusing! And Father God is not the author of that confusion. We know who is, satan, and he loves to create chaos, disruption and division. Remember that Truth as we walk through this Session together.

Where It Began

Our Church history begins with the covenant with Abraham, because we are grafted into his covenant by *believing*. Read Romans 11 for context of this grafting. It (believing) was considered unto him (Abraham) righteousness, Genesis 15:6. In the same way, by believing, we are saved and made righteous (Romans 3:22). The first mention of *righteousness* is in Genesis 15:6! Remember, first mention is critical in understanding the concept God is trying to communicate, so let's take a look at what righteousness actually means:

• Righteousness
  Strong's: H6666 *tsedaka* (Hebrew) – justice, righteousness
  G1343 *dikaiosyne* (Greek) – the state which we ought to be, acceptable to God

---

Covenant

God speaks in blood covenant language throughout the Bible. Since many of us are unfamiliar with blood covenants, let's take a quick look at the steps involved in creating one to better understand what this means and how it applies to us. (To learn more, check out *The Miracle of the Scarlet Thread*, by Richard Booker.)[3]

1. The two people exchange coats or robes. To a Hebrew, the coat or robe represented the person himself, so when he offered the other person his robe, he was offering himself – even his very life itself.

2. They take off their belt and offer it to the other person. The belt, also called the girdle, was used to hold your sword, your knife, and other fighting instruments. In this way you were saying to the other person that you were offering him your protection. If someone attacks you, they also have me to deal with. Your battles are my battles. Saul held the robes of those that stoned Stephen in Acts 7:58, so they wouldn't be known in this act. This was their identity, hidden.

3. Cut the covenant. In this part, an animal is killed and cut down the middle and the two halves are laid opposite each other. The two parties to the covenant pass between the two halves of the animal and are saying, "May God, do so to me and more if I break this covenant. This is a blood covenant and cannot be broken."

4. Raise the right arm and cut the palm of the hand and clasp each other's hand and mingle your blood. This is saying to the other person, "We are becoming one with each other." To intermingle the blood is to intermingle the very life of both people.

5. Exchange names. Each one takes part of the other's name and incorporates it into their own.

6. Make a scar or some identifying mark. The scar was the outward evidence of the covenant that others could see and know that the covenant was made. Sometimes they would rub the cut in the hand to make the scar, then anyone who wanted to fight you would know that he not only had to fight you but another as well.

7. Give terms of the covenant. Both parties to the covenant stand before a witness and list all of their assets and liabilities, because each one takes all of these upon himself. You are saying, "Everything I have is yours and everything you have is mine. If something happens to you, your covenant partner will see to it that your wife and children are taken care of."

8. Eat the memorial meal. A loaf of bread is broken in half. Each feeds his half to the other saying, "This is my body, and I am now giving it to you." Then they take wine as a symbol of his blood and says, "This is my blood which is now your blood."

9. Plant a memorial tree. The two then plant a tree as a memorial to the covenant and sprinkle it with the blood of the animal that was killed for the covenant offering.

We see all the steps of blood covenant with Abraham, and that is the covenant in which we have entered, through faith. Romans 3:30 describes this, and Romans 4 goes into more detail of the covenant of faith. John 17:2-21 talks about us as those "who believe".

It is so important to seek to understand the language of God as indicated in blood covenant language. It helps us to understand His provision and promises that we can rest upon.

In the New Covenant, the blood has been provided by Jesus as the final sacrifice, and our part to maintain relationship with the Father is to believe and then receive what He has for us, eternal life, and kingdom living. (New Testament references to Abraham: John 17:20; Romans 4:3,9,12-16, 9:30, 10:9-10; Galatians 3:6-18; Hebrews 11:8; James 2:23.)

From the formation of the New Testament Church with *Jesus building it* (Matthew 16:18), there have been multiple fractions that have brought us to this day with hundreds of church denominations, each with a different spin on what they believe. Where did this all begin?

Soon after the flood, people began to turn away from God again. In Genesis 11, the tower of Babel was created in disobedience to reach the heavens, to "make for ourselves a name" (v4).

One clear biblical example that further fractured the congregation involved Nimrod. Read Genesis 10:8 out loud; "he became" is one Hebrew word: H2490, *cha'lal*, meaning profanity, prostitute. (This is an example of how important it is to look up original language meanings.) Nimrod was key in creating and building false worship – Baal was introduced by him. Babylon and Assyria were also founded by Nimrod.

- Nimrod
  Strong's: H5428, *Nimrowd* – rebellion
  Founder of false religion. He took the name Baal (Jeremiah 23:27), which is mentioned 81 times in Bible, as a warning to all.

These fractures boil down to a desire for power and greed, to be equal to God or like God, if the root is explored. Sound familiar? The enemy does not create anything new, just twists the same lie in Genesis 3:1-6, *"Did God really mean what He said?"* This is the original sin and deception by satan of mankind. It just keeps repeating and is something to be aware of.

Church Timeline

Many big events have shaped our church history. Including the persecution by Romans (primarily Nero) of the early church, which included the martyrdom of Jesus' disciples and Paul in the first century.

- Right after Jesus' death, many of The Way were persecuted, and many by Paul himself (when he was Saul) until he was converted on the road to Damascus. Kabbala started in this timeframe as well. It was a religion in pursuit and worship of Gnosticism4 (elite knowledge).

- 321 AD – Constantine – became first Christian Emperor and changed much of the church, including:
  - Designated Sunday as the holy day of the week and incorporated Roman holidays into church calendar.
  - Our "Christian holidays" have origins in paganism, going back to Nimrod. He was a self-proclaimed savior of the people, saving people FROM God after the flood.
  - Introduced pagan symbols into the Catholic Church, ie. IHS (initials for Isis, Horus, and Siris, who are Egyptian gods) are on the cross and eucharist wafer.

- 1054 AD – The Great Schism – split the Eastern Orthodox church into the Western Roman Catholic Church.
- 1517 AD – The Reformation – Martin Luther – 99 tenants nailed to the door that we are saved by Grace, not by works.

From that point on, the division and cursing between faiths continued. There was hatred and ridicule continue over religious differences. Catholic, Protestant, Muslims, and Jewish people were all cursing one another and this continues to date.

What differentiates us – is the TRINITY – ONE God with 3 parts, Father, Son, Holy Spirit. It is fellowship that is the foundation of Christianity – Started out with Gen 1:1 – all were present at the beginning – God, Breath (Spirit) and Word (Son) John 1:1.

This fellowship then created us in their image – Gen 1:26-27. This fellowship pursues us. Any other religion demands things from those that follow them. There are tasks required to achieve certain things; there are works to do to attain and maintain status; there are things you can do to lose place in religions. All of this was met with the concept of GRACE – Christ came, settled all debts for anyone who will RECEIVE Him, and then able to walk in complete freedom.

This is the differentiator, the Trinity, desiring fellowship with us, and being WITH us. Not some high, lofty god on an altar or statue, but WITH and IN us as we receive His Holy Spirit. Receiving is the application of believing – and Jesus taught that in John 13. But that is another deep study that will be written soon!

Traditions of men have come against our identity as image bearers in the form of religious rituals, symbols, and many other things that have created chaos, division, and strife...and so many WARS that have been started because of the difference in religious beliefs!

Jesus came to unite us all in Him – we are to strive for one thing throughout the entire Bible – strive for the unity of the bond of peace between us and other believers. (Eph 4:3) Paul writes in much of Ephesians about breaking down all barriers between one another as people – and even states that to the church of Galatia – in Gal 3:28. Jesus destroyed the barriers, doing away with the wall of hostility (Eph 2:14) so that we could all be ONE. This is God's desire and one of the many reasons He sent us His Son.

Many religions have cursed other religions that do not believe what they believe. This is against Christ's teachings that we just explored. It is possible that your family line may have been affected by generational cursing by being kicked out of a church, gossiped about and wounded in that way, or removed from a leadership position because certain "works" were not accomplished. Whatever the wound, this is easily healed (generationally!!) by praying aloud this simple prayer:

I choose to forgive (name religion, person or community) for cursing me and my ancestors. I break the purpose and power of these curses for me and my family line, including my children, grandchildren and all descendants. I ask for forgiveness for my part in this and I receive Your forgiveness, Lord. I ask for complete restoration of all that was lost or stolen because of these curses. I appropriate (take it and make it mine) the finished work of the Cross of Christ Jesus here, too, in my life and the lives of my descendants. I pray all of this in the holy Name of Jesus Christ of Nazareth.

As we have learned from the small portion of Christian History we have discussed, there is a *full-on assault* against the Church from the beginning – and it continues. We have an enemy, the ruler of this world, and he knows his end is near. He knows what the Bible says – Jesus WINS!

Do not lose heart!

Warned in the Bible – We Are to Be Aware

We are warned over and over in the Bible about false teachers, false doctrines, and corruption. Read these together and make note of what each verse says:

1. Matthew 21:33-45

2. Matthew 23:2-33 (What does Jesus say about leaders specifically?)

3. Matthew 7:15, 24:11, 24:24

4. Mark 13:22

31

5. 2 Thessalonians 2:9-11

6. 2 Timothy 3:1-9

7. 1 John 4:1

How do we make sense of all this history and follow Jesus as commanded? It is boiled down simply for us by Christ Himself in Matthew 22:37-40. Read this out loud.

Next, read 1 Timothy 4 and make a list of what it looks like to live out the godly life:

Spend some time in prayer and ask the Lord what else He wants you to know about how to live as a believer?

How are we to know true worship and true religion? Read the following verses out loud and write down your observations.

- True Worship (John 4:23; Philippians 3:3)

- True Religion (James 1:27)

I have experienced tremendous warfare in the church organizations I have belonged to. I used to be hurt and angry at the "perpetrators" of these wounds, but I now know that there is ultimately one responsible for the continuous assault on Jesus' Church: satan himself. We will learn more about warfare in the next session.

Wrap Up Questions

1. How have you personally experienced this assault of the Church, as a member of the Body?

2. What is God showing you about this (these) experiences?

3. How will you respond to this revelation? Record what you hear from Him.

4. What is becoming clearer for you?

5. What is the most important take away for you from this weeks' time in the Word?

Additional Notes:

Spiritual Warfare

Spiritual Warfare and Conflict in the Church

In the many years I have been involved in church life, I have experienced much warfare and many conflicts. I would imagine each of you have as well. My hope in including this topic in this Study is to bring this concept out into the light. I have been in very difficult circumstances where leadership was trying to control me, and even went as far as to state that I needed to check with him before anyone else in my life about a ministry idea, because he was my "covering". I was also told by him that disobedience to this could lead to bad things happening to my children. This was not even two years after my son died in a traumatic car accident. This would fit into the category of spiritual abuse. However, I didn't realize that until much later, and after seeking counseling to heal.

This type of control is found in some church organizations, sadly. Through some time of healing prayer and processing these things, I have learned the power of forgiveness, and the healing continues as the Lord leads me forward on His path for me. If you feel like you have experienced some spiritual abuse, I recommend seeking wise, Christian counseling to explore the healing process available to you as well. I do not want to make light of this, as it can be very devastating. It takes time to heal.

Now that we are in Session Four, we are deepening our Biblical understanding about what the Church is, the purpose of the Church, and some Church history. This is all leading us into a better understanding of God's design for the Church and our part in that design.

We are now entering into the Session where we will look at the spiritual warfare and conflict in the church.

We Have an Enemy

Let's discuss and define satan's role in the Bible. Read through Ezekiel 28, Isaiah 14, and Revelation 12:7-17 out loud.

- What is satan's response to being cast down?

- What is changing about your beliefs about when bad things happen to good people?

Let's define and explore *persecution*:

- Persecution
  Strong's: G1377, *dioko* – to suffer, to mistreat, harass, to chase, to cause to run.

- What stirs in you when you hear this word, or think about *persecution* as a believer?

- In Revelation 12:13 & 17 satan *persecutes* the Church. What's becoming clear for you right now?

Now let's look at God's involvement when there are *trials and tribulation* in Job's life. Read Job 1 & 2 out loud.

- What does this provoke in you?

- Read Job 38 & 39 out loud (read this with attitude!) as God was responding to Job and his friends. What does this mean?

- Read Job 41 out loud about restoration. What does this do for you in light of your current circumstances where you are experiencing/have experienced suffering?

Let's see what the Bible says about angels:

- What is their job? Read Hebrews 1:1-14 out loud. Write down some things you learned about angels.

Verses About Persecution

The Bible has a lot to say about understanding persecution. To gain a deeper understanding, here are some verses to explore.

Read	What did you learn?
Psalms 34:19	
Psalms 119:71	
Job 13:15	
Isaiah 43:2	
Matthew 4:1-17	
Matthew 5:10-12	
Matthew 10:38	
Matthew 13:21	
Luke 14:27	
John 16:33	
Acts 8:1-3	
Romans 5:3-5, 8:18,	
1 Corinthians 10:13	
2 Corinthians 1:3-7	
2 Corinthians 11:16-33	
2 Corinthians 12:10	
Philippians 1:29, 3:10	
Colossians 1:24	
2 Thessalonians 1:4	
2 Timothy 2:3-4	
2 Timothy 3:11-12	
Hebrews 2:10-11	
James 1:2-4, 12	
1 Peter 1:6-7	
1 Peter 2:19-21	
1 Peter 3:14	
1 Peter 4:12-19	
1 Peter 5:10	

Verses About Enduring

When we face persecution, there is a command to *endure*. What does that look like?

- Endure

  Strong's: G5278, *hupomeno* – to choose to stay under extreme pressure

What does this produce in us as the Church? Read the following verses out loud and record what you learn.

Read	What did you learn?
Luke 21:19	
2 Corinthians 6:4	
Hebrews 10:36	
Hebrews 12:1	
James 1:3-4	
James 5:11	

Reflection Questions

1. What have you always believed about persecution? Did that belief change after studying the Bible about this topic?

2. What is the fruit or outworking of persecution?

3. Where do you see this in your life?

4. How is your perspective on persecution changing right now?

Let's keep pursuing this and see what else we can learn about this!

I love to use the Greek word, *hupomeno*, as a verb: *hupomeno*-ing. Try it, it's fun to say! Read Hebrews 12:2 out loud. How did Jesus *hupomeno*?

Read the following out loud and write what you learn.

1. Matthew 10:12

2. Romans 12:12

3. 2 Timothy 2:12

4. Hebrews 12:7

5. James 1:12

6. 1 Peter 2:20

What does this enduring, or *hupomeno*-ing, produce in us as the Church? What is the fruit? List what you learn about the results:

"Consider it all joy... when you come under fiery ordeals...", James 1:2 says. Wait, *what?!?!*

Now how do you view that verse, after understanding the fruit that God is after?

New science has proven that choosing joy is fuel to heal your brain from much, including trauma.[6]

Personal Warfare

We will experience warfare, and Paul speaks to this. It is not against people (even in the church!), but against spiritual powers and principalities. But we are not left without weapons to defend ourselves, that enable us to stand firm.

1. Armor of God (Read Ephesians 6:10-17 & 2 Corinthians 10:4 out loud)
   • Why do we need this? What does Paul say about battles in these verses?

   • List the commands in Ephesians 6:10-17. What are you learning in this?

2. Awareness

- John 10:10 says, "The thief comes only to steal and kill and destroy. [Christ] came that [we] may have life and have it abundantly."
- 1 John 3:8 says, "Jesus came to destroy the works of the devil."
- 1 Peter 5:8 says, "Be of sober spirit, be alert. Your adversary, the devil, prowls around, like a lion, seeking someone to devour."

3. Authority *(Exousia)* and Power *(Dunamis)*

Read 2 Corinthians 10:1-4 out loud. These weapons are " divinely powerful", or some versions have "mighty before God" to describe the weapons we have! Let's look at some of them:

---

a. Authority

Strong's: G1849, *exousia* – authority of power, jurisdiction, delegated influence

---

- Read Revelation 2:26-29. *Authority* is given to the churches because of Revelation 12:11. Read this out loud, as this is key – overcoming involves the word of our testimony!

- Read Mark 3:15 and 16:17 out loud. This is *authority* in action: casting out demons as a sign to unbelievers.

- Read Matthew 28:18-20 out loud. Jesus has all *authority*, and He is with us, until the end of the age.

- Read John 14:12 out loud. What does this look like?

- Be alert – 1 Peter 5:8 & John 10:10 – So that we can exercise our *authority* we have in Christ Jesus over the enemy

---

b. Power
    Strong's: G1411, *dunamis* – miraculous power, strength and might resting upon armies, hosts

---

- Jesus came with *power* and *authority*. Read out loud: Luke 4:36, 9:1 & 10:19.

- Acts 1:8 promises power when the Holy Spirit comes. What are you beginning to realize?

4. Prayer is a great weapon! Bold prayer is what the Church does. See examples all through Scripture, but here are two:

    - Daniel prayed three times a day when it was against the law! Daniel 10:12-13 explains the warfare that goes on in the heavenlies regarding our prayers.

    - Peter was in prison in Acts 12 and the church prayed fervently for his release. See Acts 12:5 and notice what happened to Peter in this story – miraculous release!

Prayer is very powerful, and we are to pray boldly as a Church. See Appendix B for *Daily Prayer* by John Eldredge.

5. Praying in the Name of Jesus. Why do we do this? Let's look at the root of the word, *name*.

   • Name
   Strong's: G368, *onoma*
   Derivative of G1097, *ginosko* – to know
   And of G3685, *onemei* – to receive profit or advantage, to be helped

   • Praying in the Name of Jesus is knowing that He is our best and only source of help! Let this sink in. We are commanded to bless His Name, and His Name has power. 1 Chronicles 23:13, John 20:31 & Acts 3:16. Even the Pharisees knew the power of His Name in Acts 5:40!

Fear

"Do not be afraid," occurs 365 times in the Bible, one for each day. Is that a coincidence? We have not been given a spirit of fear, but of power, love and discipline (sound mind) – from 2 Timothy 1:7. Fear tries to separate us from God (as sin – first mentioned in Genesis 4:7) but fear is a spirit that comes against us. Read that again. I now recognize this truth, and look for what fear itself is afraid of, and can usually get immediate clarity.

Battles in the Church

Remember the importance of the Ministry of Reconciliation steps (Matthew 18) from Session One?
What do you believe about quarrels in church among believers? What is changing about this belief?

The enemy has a special hatred for the Church, because Jesus loves the Church, as His *bride*. We want to be aware of the spiritual battle that is
ongoing over the Church. This is not a new battle, but can take on different forms, to appear personal to us.

What are you beginning to notice about Spiritual Warfare?

- In your personal life?

- In your family?

- In your church body?

Wrap Up Questions

1. What revelations are you beginning to have about the Church?

2. How will you respond to warfare with these new revelations?

Additional Notes:

SESSION FIVE

One Anothers

"You cannot hope to give to others what you have not received yourself...
One anothering begins on the inside."
Authentic Relationships

– Wayne Jacobson,

"To love one another is to see the face of God."

– Les Misérables

We Are Vital to Each Other!

I have truly enjoyed the deep friendships that the Lord has given me in other believers. There is something different about those relationships, as we have Jesus, Love Himself, in the midst of us. These One Anothers have been lifelines when I have needed them in times of intense grief and pain, as well as celebrating with the joy of heaven together when there are breakthroughs and answer to prayers. Some of the darkest times in my life, like the diagnosis of my youngest with cystic fibrosis, and the death of my oldest son, have been wrapped in the loving presence of One Anothers. The joy of dancing with my middle son at his wedding was also shared by significant One Anothers. Burdens are divided and joys are multiplied. I *love* God's math!

We have studied about the biblically defined "what" of Church in Old Testament and the New Testament, the history of the Church, spiritual warfare in the Church and our role, and now we are going to look at the "how" as described in the Word of God. I have learned so much about God from other people in my life. Over the years I have had friends point me to God in so many ways. Gently correcting me, encouraging me, sponsoring me to a retreat when we had no extra money to spare, and walking with me in my deepest, darkest days of grief. Without One Anothers I would not have had the opportunity to get to know Jesus, the Holy Spirit, and the Father so intimately!

As a member of the Body, each of us is a very vital component to be used by God to minister to the world AND to our One Anothers.

We are all Ministers of Reconciliation (2 Corinthians 5:18) and it is an essential action that we are called to, for the health of the Church, which is US!

We were created by a Fellowship for fellowship, or relationship, in the image of God, the Triune Fellowship. Read Genesis 1:26 out loud.

God speaks to Groups. His covenant language is with people groups (Genesis 10:5, 12:2, 22:18) and we are the seed/descendants of Abraham, as determined in Session Three. All through Scripture we are referred to as descendants of Abraham.

God expects us to operate in covenant with Him and with each other. There is much that can be learned about covenants, but that is another study which I would encourage you to pursue on your own!

What Does This Look Like on a Daily Basis?

How do we *do* Church and *be* Church?

The Church is a gathering of believers that is a safe place to fall - a safe place to rest, a safe place to be with those that love like Jesus loves.

We have also explored the gifts that we are to employ to use in the Church, to help the common good. We are to act like Jesus to our fellow members, as explained in 1 Corinthians 12:1-14:40.

The Fruit of the Spirit

Let's discuss these in context. *This* is Church living, and the living Church!!!

We are known by our fruit. How does one bear these fruits? Read Matthew 12:33 out loud and discuss.

I like to say "fruit happens" when we are walking with the Fruit-giver, the Spirit of God. We cannot manifest, strive, work on, or produce any of these fruits. We can only receive them from the Holy Spirit!

The fruit of the Spirit is Love, Joy, Peace, Patience, Goodness, Kindness, Faithfulness, Gentleness, and Self Control. We are to live and WALK by the Spirit (Galatians 5:25).

Who are my One Anothers?

• Anothers
  Strong's: H251, *ach* – brother
  G240 *allelon* – another, others, themselves, yourselves.
  This is a plural of G243, *allos* – adjective-another, other

From Vine's Expository Dictionary (Vine's is a dictionary that cross references key words in Hebrew and Greek and can provide some context for the culture): "The word *allos* expresses a numerical difference and denotes 'another of the same sort.' The word *allelon* is a reciprocal pronoun in the genitive plural, signifying 'of, or from, one another' (akin to *allos*, "another"), e.g., Matthew 25:32; John 13:22; Acts 15:39, 19:38; 1 Corinthians 7:5; Galatians 5:17."[7]

What this is saying is that One Anothering is a process of building relationship and deepening of intimacy with fellow believers. It is a journey of becoming more like Jesus every day, together in community.

Twenty "One Anothers" Commands

Here are just some of the One Anothering verses. Let's explore these and record what we learn in the list below:

Verse	Action	Where or Who?
John 13:34	Love	
Romans 12:10	Be devoted to & honor	
Romans 12:16	Be of the same mind	
Romans 15:7, 14	Accept & instruct	
Galatians 5:13	Carry burdens	
Ephesians 4:2	Bear with	
Ephesians 4:7	Forgive	
Ephesians 4:32	Be Kind	
Ephesians 5:21	Submit	
Colossians 3:16	Admonish	
1 Thess 4:18, 2 Cor 1	Comfort	
1 Thessalonians 5:11	Build up	
Hebrews 3:13	Encourage daily	
Hebrews 10:24	Stimulate to love and good deeds	
Hebrews 13:16	Share with	
James 5:16	Pray & confess to one another	
1 Peter 4:9	Be hospitable	

Forgiving Ourselves

Let's also remember that WE are included in this list as "each others".

Ephesians 4:32, "Be kind to one another, tender hearted, forgiving each other, just as God in Christ also has forgiven you."

Colossians 3:13, "Bearing with one another and forgiving each other, whoever has a complaint against anyone; just as the Lord forgave you, so also should you."

- Each Other

Strong's: 1438, *heautou* – oneself, himself/herself, yourselves

What is coming to mind as you think about self-forgiveness? Take a moment and spend time with the Father right now to take care of that unfinished business.

Father, forgive me for holding onto unforgiveness against myself for _____. I now see that as sin that separates me from You. I receive Your forgiveness and break the power of that circumstance in my life. I choose to receive all You have for me around this. (Write down anything you sense, hear, see.)

Wrap Up Questions

1. As we process these commands (yes, we are *commanded* to do these One Anothers), what is changing for you personally?

2. How do you see yourself in these verses? How have you experienced some "one anothering" at the hand of another believer?

3. What was the most significant revelation to you in this session's material?

4. What action step are you committed to taking after this Session Five time of study? Write it down:

Additional Notes:

SESSION SIX

Let the Healing Come

Let the Healing Come... and Continue

We have explored the truth about Church wounds extensively throughout our time together. In this time, we have built some relationships and cultivated them by sharing some of our lives with our One Anothers. Last Session, we dug deeply into the definition of our One Anothers and how we build, deepen, and fortify those relationships by "doing life" together more intimately.

We have ventured into the area of Church history and how it has been ravaged by the enemy. We looked at the purpose of the Church, and our specific, beautifully choreographed part to play in it by using our gifts, calling, and desires for the Church. We now know that *we are the Church*, and we are *responsible* to be and do all that we do... as that Church.

We also clarified the warfare that is ongoing, and how we might be effective against that warfare in the local organized Church as well as the larger Church. We have access to weapons that are not of this world. We have access to the Lord God Almighty, the commander of the angel armies.

This Session, we are exploring the healing process, as defined by Jesus. At His coming, many rejoiced because they knew He would deliver them from their circumstances and provide everlasting life. Hosanna in Hebrew means, "SAVE US!!!" This is how He was received into Jerusalem on Palm

Sunday. When He died, many were shocked and in disbelief. This tragedy, experienced by His followers, ended up being revealed as the greatest gift ever to be known.

In this time of healing together, we will each share a bit about the wounding we have experienced and ask Jesus to come and heal this. In some circumstances, it may be helpful to have someone sit in for that person who was used to hurt you and ask for forgiveness on behalf of/in place of that person. This is a powerful method of being able to hear those words, "I am sorry I hurt you. Can you please forgive me?" There is no pressure to do so, but it is highly encouraged, so that you can fully experience the healing Jesus died to give you. Your heart matters to Him, and He already knows the wounds you have suffered and have been carrying around with you. I want to assure you that in your boldness, peace will be renewed.

Jesus Came to Heal the Broken Hearted

Read Psalms 147:3, Isaiah 61:1, and Luke 4:18 out loud.

He came to save *all* that was lost (Matthew 18:11)... not just *who* was lost. To save (*sozo* in the Greek) means to save, heal, deliver, restore, and make whole.

How would you define your "heart"? Discuss.

What does the Bible say about our hearts? The first mention of the word heart is in Genesis 6:5, just before the flood. Read this verse out loud.

- Heart
  Strong's: H3820, *leb* (Hebrew) – inner man, mind, will, our soul
  G2588– *kardia* (Greek) – heart, center of our being, our
  innermost part, seat of emotions, will, mind, our soul

God's heart is mentioned in Genesis 6:6, where it says that God was sorry that He had made man, and in His heart, He was grieved.

The same word is used for God's heart and for our heart. What does that stir in you?

In Hebrew, the word for heart is *leb*, and is interchanged with and used as proper pronouns for God and for His people. Our heart and God's heart are important and are referenced many times in Scripture. Below are a few to give you an idea of what God wants us to know.

1. Genesis 8:21 – God, Himself

2. Genesis 27:41 – Esau, himself

3. Genesis 50:21 – Joseph, spoke kindly to his brothers (from his inner being)

Read the following verses below out loud and discuss what you learned about your heart:

1. Romans 10:8 – *the word* is in our hearts

2. Romans 10:9-10 – it is with our hearts *we believe*

3. Galatians 4:6 – the *Spirit of Christ is in* our hearts

4. Ephesians 3:17 – *Christ dwells* in our heart

5. Ephesians 6:22 – our hearts *need comforting* at times

6. Philippians 4:6-7 – When we bring all our needs to God, peace *guards* our hearts and minds in Christ Jesus

7. Colossians 2:2, 4:8 – our hearts *need encouraging*

8. Colossians 3:15 – we are to let the peace of Christ *rule* in our hearts.

- Rule
  Strong's: G1013, *brabeuo* – to control, be an umpire, decide, determine

---

9. 1 Thessalonians 2:4 – God examines our hearts

10. 1 Thessalonians 3:13 – Jesus establishes our hearts without blame in love

---

- Establish
  Strong's: G4841 sterizo – to make firm, strengthen, set fast, render constant, make stable

---

11. 2 Thessalonians 2:16-17 – Jesus strengthens our hearts and comforts us

12. 2 Thessalonians 3:5 – the Lord directs our heart into love of God and steadfastness of Jesus

13. Hebrews 10:16 – the new covenant laws are written on our hearts and minds

Commands of What *Not* to Do with Our Hearts

Here are some verses to read out loud that have instructions about what *not* to do with our hearts:

1. John 14:1, 27 – Do not let your heart be _____ nor let it be _____.

2. John 12:40

3. Acts 7:51 – Stephen's sermon: stiff-necked and _____ hearts, always resisting the Holy Spirit.

4. 2 Corinthians 4:1, 16 – Since we have _____ and _____ we do not lose heart.

5. Hebrews 3:8,15, 4:7

6. James 4:8

Hardened Hearts

Let's look more deeply at *hardening* or *hardened hearts*. The first mention of this is in Exodus 4:14 where the Lord is telling Moses He will cause Pharaoh's heart to be hardened.

- Hardened
  Strong's: H2388, *chazaq* – to bind to tie, to fortify, to strengthen.

What are the consequences of a *hardened heart*?

Now, let's see what happened to Pharaoh and his people. Take turns reading Exodus 14:17-31 out loud. What did you learn in this story?

The New Testament talks about the consequences of a *hardened heart* too. Read the following verses and write what you learn.

- John 12:40

- Ephesians 4:18

How might you apply this awareness of your heart to your own circumstances right now?

Your Story

All of your circumstances create the chapters of your story. What you are experiencing right now is a part of your future. God uses all things together for good for those that are called according to His purposes (Romans 8:28).

Are you able to see a place in your life where there was a difficult, even painful, time when you can now look back and see how God is using *THAT* circumstance for His glory and His good? Take some time right now to reflect a bit and write it down here to remember:

The reason this Bible study is in your hands is because of the pain of being repeatedly wounded *IN* the church by fellow believers. I am proof that God uses things for His glory. I can now celebrate that by knowing this study guide is in your hands and that which was meant for evil, is now being used for good (Genesis 50:20).

Healing the Brokenhearted

Brokenhearted is different than hardened heart. It is a word used only three times in the Bible in this form, but the Hebrew word is translated into broken, shattered, crushed, smashed, etc, multiple times.

- Brokenhearted
  Strong's: H7665, *shabar* – to break into pieces, shatter, rupture, wrend violently, wreck

I have felt this type of pain in my heart and physically at many times in my life: When my dad left on Christmas when I was age 5; when we moved cross country in the middle of the night, and I couldn't say goodbye to friends at age 12; when someone I trusted was unfaithful; when a friend turned on me in rage at her wedding as maid of honor... so many times of my heart breaking... and me bravely scooping it up, holding it together, and giving it out again only to have it dropped repeatedly, shattered. I have since learned my whole heart of trust is given only to Father God. He protects it (Proverbs 3:5-6).

Have you felt your heart feel these things? Jesus knows this happens, and THIS IS what He came for (Psalms 147:3). He came to heal the brokenhearted.

- Heal/ Healing
  Strong's: H7495, *raphe* (Hebrew) – to heal, make whole, to mend by stitching, cure, heal thoroughly
  G2323, *therapeuo* (Greek) – to heal, cure, worship

More verses on healing:

- Psalms 41:4 – David knew his *soul* needed healing.

- Luke 9:1 – Jesus gave the disciples power and authority over all demonic and to heal diseases

- Acts 5:16 – The New Testament church – healing of unclean spirits

- Acts 28:27 – We can be healed of dull hearts

- What areas of your heart have been wounded and how? This is a time to share with your group in a way that is honoring to the person or organization used "unwittingly" by the enemy to wound you.

Forgiveness

Here are some things to remember and be aware of as you choose to set your will with God's will and choose to forgive.

1. The enemy cannot have a place unless we give it to him (Ephesians 4:27).
   • Place
     Strong's: G5117, *topos* – place; where we get topography

2. Satan is an opportunist and when we give place to him, he will take us up on it 100% of the time. In the state of unforgiveness, he lies to us and wants us to hold onto that for power, control, or a multitude of other lies. Forgiveness is a simple choice to obey. The word "unforgiveness" is not in the Bible, but the word "offense" is, and that Greek word (G4624) is *skandalon*, and is a TRAP.

3. We learned in Session Five that forgiveness is a command, and unforgiveness means we will be turned over to the tormentors (Matthew 18:34). If you have been feeling tormented and tortured, this could be a big reason.

Healing Prayer Time – Facilitated by Group Leader

How would it look to have Jesus heal these areas for you?

Would you be willing to invite Jesus to heal those areas of your heart that have been wounded? Let's take a look at one method of inner healing prayer, called Identificational Forgiveness. Below are the steps to follow. It is important that these words are spoken out loud. Take the time your group needs for anyone who wants to do these steps.

1. One person "stands in" for the person that was used to wound you. The stand in person asks for your forgiveness, and then speaks words of affirmation over you (words that you may have longed to hear.)

   For example: I am sorry I didn't value your gifts more. I trust your heart is good. I know that you have value, and your talents are very useful for kingdom work.

2. You then choose to forgive and release the real person (by name, if possible), breaking all unholy bonds with that person, releasing them to Jesus.

Example of confession/forgiveness:

I confess my sin of agreeing with the lie that I (state the lie), and I choose to forgive those that helped me form this lie or contributed to it in any way. I choose to forgive: (list anyone who you'd like to forgive, by name, if possible).

I ask forgiveness for believing this lie and living my life based upon it. I receive Your forgiveness, Father.

I choose to forgive myself as well, because You have forgiven me.

I break the power of this lie, and renounce any and all power the enemy and his demonic forces have had in my life....and in the lives of my descendants.

3. Next, replace the lies with the truth.

    I ask You, Father, for Your truth. What do You say? (Take a quiet moment to listen to what you hear in your heart/spirit and write it down here.)

4. Break all ungodly ties with this person and declare that they owe you nothing. Jesus paid the debt and expectations are transferred to Jesus.

    I break all ungodly soul ties with _____ and choose to forgive them. _____ owes me nothing, and I transfer all of my expectations to Jesus.

This is a very powerful step you just took. Take a moment to assess how you feel. What do you notice physically? What do you notice emotionally?

There is a larger Story that is going on and you play an integral part in that Story, with your story. John Eldredge speaks to this in his book, *Epic.* He reflects that our hearts are stirred in stories and movies that have a villain and a hero and all is well at the end, as that is OUR story, and God's story. Your story matters and is key for kingdom-living purposes in the lives around you (James 1:2).

Be sure to share what God has done - as we overcome by the blood of the lamb and the word of our testimony. We were created to glorify Him. Have fun deciding what to do and who to share this freedom with in the next couple of days!

Celebration!

Your group may want to plan a celebration meal together!

Congratulations!

Y ou have completed a big step in this journey toward more healing in your life by making it this far in this study. God is all about healing, when we let Him.

This may be the first step for you, or it may be a reminder of things at the wounding has caused you to forget. Wherever you are in your journey, you are headed forward and into the "more", that abundant life, that Jesus came to give you here, now (John 10:10).

We are commanded to celebrate! Celebrations are all over in the Bible in many illustrations. It is something the Lord does, and we get to join Him!

The first time the word *celebrate* is used is during the Passover (Exodus 5:1). Moses is being instructed on all the details of the Passover, a permanent ordinance, something we do for forever. Our New Testament Passover is communion – we are to remember we have been saved by the blood (Luke 22:15-20). We will be having communion today as a group, to celebrate this great healing and deliverance journey we have been on together with the Father.

We celebrate the awareness of being restored to the Father and His goodness. It is true, and forever will be, that "He is good, and His lovingkindness is everlasting". The Hebrew word for *lovingkindness* is *hesed* and is defined as a lavish, kind, encompassing love. The kind of love that draws you up into His lap and into His arms to receive.

This *hesed* love is an attachment to God. Attachment love is what is needed for us to be able to experience Love Himself. Who are we attached to? This is a newly discovered connection to our brains, our minds, and to love. Neuroscience allows us to see, literally, the effects of this love on our brains through functional MRIs (fMRI). This choice to love is an act of abiding, surrendering, receiving, and a sense of safety to be in His love.

Our identity is formed by whom we love. This has been explored by neuroscience, and the newly forming neurotheology field is beginning to discover how we attach to God through LOVE. The Greek word for love, in verb form, is *agapeo*, when quoting, "love your neighbor as yourself".

This Greek word is the combination of the Hebrew word used most often for love, *aheb*, and lovingkindness, *hesed*. So, this love is not just a command, it is an expression of our new identity in Christ as a believer that has been born from above (born again).

Now that you have an awareness of the truth about the healing of wounds you have received in the church setting[8] (the organization and human part of church) I want to celebrate that with you. These wounds are evidence of areas of your gifting and areas of strength that you possess for Kingdom purposes. Think about that. When we think about warfare, what does the enemy strike at first? Weaknesses or strengths? What is more dangerous to the enemy? Have these assaults that you've experienced been directed at your strengths, areas of giftedness, and calling?

As a believer, you are the Church. You have a calling and a purpose. You are a minister and have assignments to complete. This assault has been an attempt to derail you.

I would venture to guess that if you were to chronicle the hurts you have experienced at the hands of believers, or leadership in church, that you could see a pattern. I challenge you to look upon those circumstances with fresh, healing eyes, and ask the Lord what He wants to show you.

You have something that is dangerous to the enemy, and he's been after it for a long time. His goal has been to sideline you, take you out of the game, and keep you impotent. Your area of hurt is actually an area of powerful Kingdom assignment.

As you process that statement, what are your noticing happening within you? Take that energy, that passion and decide how you will now use your gifting.

1. How will you strengthen and fortify this area of your life?

2. Where do you feel God wants you to use this gift/talent for His purposes?

3. Who will you connect with to help with accountability in this journey?

4. What is true about you in this area of gifting?

As I have walked into more freedom and used all the hurts, including my "church wounds" to write this study, it is a celebration of so much of what God has done. This is a glimpse into how we can "consider it all joy" when we go through hard things. Because HE USES them all! As I walk this out and learn to see the enemy's assaults for what they truly are – a feeble attempt to take me out of the game – I can continue to stand and encourage others to do the same.

The Church is the Bride of Christ and soon there will be a Wedding Feast like none we could ever imagine. I look forward to that celebration when it comes and until then, we get to celebrate a little bit of that joy here. We have journeyed through a study together and learned much about God's heart for His Church. His heart is good and for you, and His love is everlasting. These are the things He wants you to always remember. This is the unity of the faith.

You have newfound freedom and have claimed literal territory/space back from the enemy. Again, remember how you physically feel after choosing to forgive someone and let the Lord heal those locked up places. Remember not to give the devil opportunity, translated *place* in Greek (Ephesians 4:27).

My prayer for each of you is that you can now clearly see the true enemy and see the assault that has been launched on the Church by satan himself.

With God's help, you will prevail and not let the enemy have another moment of your time regarding this offense. The Holy Spirit will make you more sensitive to the enemy's attempts, and it will become easier and easier to resist him. When you submit to God, satan has to flee (James 4:7).

You are now walking in more freedom that will allow you clarity and visibility to be able to sense the attack and deal with it appropriately. You can use the authority of Jesus' name, blood, and the given authority you have as a believer in Him and His finished work on the cross.

Remember to put on the Armor of God (Ephesians 6:10-17) and operate from that place of enlistment. Standing firm, alert, and aware of the enemy's schemes. You are in the army of God, and the armor is clearly marked and identifiable by the enemy. And the Lord has your back (Isaiah 58:8).

This season of wounding, retreating, and healing has not been a waste. God is using this too for His purposes. We can trust that, because His Word says that (Romans 8:28).

I would like to encourage you to do something that is memorable to mark this date/time. Do a project, a piece of art, a journal entry, plant a tree or a bush to remember this time, and to remind you of the amazing heart God has for you. He is for you and when that is realized, we get to apply this Scripture:

The Lord is for me; I will not fear. What can man do to me?
– Psalms 118:6

Now What? How to Continue in This Healing Journey

You have stayed in this small group of One Anothers and have persevered through some areas of wounding that have long kept you from things that are yours: relationships, tasks, assignments, and destiny. My hope is that you have gained some insight, some clarity, and received healing and restoration in areas of your life that were long dormant, tucked away from further possible hurt.

Now is the time – *now* is when you get to move forward into what He has for you. Romans 11:29 says as much: the gifts of God are irrevocable. So now, what will you do with this newly found freedom, this truth about His Church, and the days you have before you?

1. Everything we need to live the life God intends is in His word. It is when we deviate from that model, that blueprint that He designed, that we find ourselves living the "less than" life!

2. **Take Courage.** Moving forward in the healing you have received takes courage. We get to take that courage from Jesus. In every instance in the Bible, the Old Testament and the New Testament, "taking courage" is an indicator of receiving, and it's receiving from the Lord. In the New Testament, Jesus says to "take courage" seven times. For further study, look them up and notice the context of what is happening, where courage is needed. (Matthew 9:2, 9:22, 14:27; Mark 6:50, 10:49; John 16:33; Acts 23:11.)

3. **Faith.** Believing. The covenant we enter into with the Father through belief (read Genesis 15, John 17, and James 2:23). We have entered this covenant of righteousness through belief and are prayed for by Jesus in John 17:20. We are also a friend of God, like Abraham (James 2:23). Let that soak deeply into your spirit. You. Are. A. Friend. Of the most high God!!!

4. **Hope.** Faith and hope are closely linked together. There is much to learn about hope in the Word of God. Hebrews 11:1 talks about this close connection of faith and hope. Our hope is IN Christ.

In Romans 8:24, it is defined as a Greek word meaning both creation and confidence. When you are feeling less than hopeful, press into reading the scriptures about hope! When it feels like you've lost hope, seek it out. Romans 15:13 is a wonderful encouragement too!

5. **Two commandments.** They summarize the law that Jesus came to fulfill. The ten commandments were broken up into two halves, the first five were laws about relationship with God and the last five were about relationship with others. Jesus stated this simply to us all: Love God and love one another. Have some fun and study the words for love in Old and New Testaments – write and share what you learn!

6. **Preach the whole gospel.** Acts 20:24. We do not want to omit anything about the message of the gospel. As the Church, we are the ones to bring this good news to the hurting, broken, angry world. This whole gospel includes the reality of being indwelt by the living, Holy God with His Spirit. Having the Holy Spirit in us, at all times, gives us so much *power* and *authority* – that which Jesus *DIED* to give to us as His bride. Ephesians 1: 18-23 spells this out clearly. We need to pray this prayer over ourselves and our Church, as this is God's desire.

7. **Operate in the given power and authority.** Luke 10:17-24 is where Jesus talks about this. The 70 came back amazed that they were able to have authority to cast out demons and evil spirits by His name. He gave them all authority over the serpent and the enemy. He said not to rejoice in that – but to be blessed that they have seen things that kings and prophets have longed to see.

8. **Share.** Share what have you experienced in this time of intentional exploration of wounding and healing. Let others know what God has done! It builds your faith, gives other hope, and most importantly brings glory to the Father!

- 1 Peter 3:15. Revere Christ in your heart and always be ready to share the reason for the hope within you. What is your story of encountering Jesus? Think on that, write it down, and share it with others when they ask. Your story is so powerful!

- Revelation 12:11. We are saved by the blood of the lamb, but we overcome by the word of our testimony. We must tell of what God has done in our lives! I love to get together with other believers and ask a simple conversation starter, "What has God been showing you lately?" or, "What have you noticed God doing in your life?" These are ways to learn together, build community, be of "one mind" as a body, and to bring God glory. We were made for this type of community and sharing of the great things of our Father!

9. **Be on guard/alert/aware.** Luke 21:34-36. Pray! Pray the Daily Prayer, included in Appendix B.

10. **Pay attention to your heart.** It is the wellspring of life. Guard it! Proverbs 4:23. Do a word search on heart and see how important our heart is!

11. **Armor of God.** Ephesians 6:10-17. Know that in Jesus, you are armored up and able to stand. You do not need to mount up, draw your sword and charge into battle. You are called to just stand. That we can do.

12. **Communion.** Remembering all Jesus has given you! As you study the in Christ verses in Appendix A, make a list of everything you get to walk in because of Jesus. Luke 22. Take communion often to remember these things. We are to remember what He has already done for us! Ephesians 1:3 says we have already been given every spiritual blessing in Christ. And of course, every blessing we

need is spiritual, because Father God is spiritual! Take a moment out of your day, get a beverage and a chip/cracker/whatever you may have on hand, and sit, pray, and remember all Jesus did for you, and partake of this meal of peace. This is the meal offering, the last of the optional sacrifices that the Lord set up in the Old Testament. It is the celebration of the intimacy we get to have with the Father! Jesus fulfilled all the required sacrifices for us (sin offering and trespass offering) and the other three offerings are our options to walk with the Father more closely. He hopes at we choose to! Communion is the meal offering; do it as often as you drink and eat to remember. Jesus said so in Luke 22. (Read more about this in *The Miracle of the Scarlet Thread*, by Richard Booker.³)

13. **Community.** One Anothers: we are created for community, to live together to be the body (His Church) together. (For another great study, look up all the verses with "One Another" using *blueletterbible.org*.)

14. **Kingdom Living.** The "how" to be the Church for believers and a hurting world – the kingdom of God is mentioned so many times in Luke. Read this gospel and make a list of all the things that you learn about the Kingdom of God. I have a friend that has written a new book that is coming out from her years of teaching about Kingdom Living: *It's Time for a Revolution*, by Dr. Jessica Rothmeyer. Watch for it!!

15. **Living by the Spirit.** Being aware and submitted to God, as that is where we are able to receive the abundant life, by abiding in Him. We can also sense warfare and quickly respond using the authority and power we have in Christ. We can do this for ourselves, and for others. James 4:7. This place of active submission is the safest place to be, and it is the definition of abiding.

16. **Wounds.** We can lead *with* wounds, but not from them. Jesus came to bind up the brokenhearted and to heal our wounds. Why

is this? Because He knew the enemy would be cruel and seek to destroy us. AND He also knew our wounds are powerful places for testimony. Genesis 50:20 is one of my favorite verses in my life. This book was birthed from that verse and the story of Joseph redeeming the lives of those who had sought to kill him. We must first experience the brokenness to experience the miraculous healing God has for each of us. We can then lead those around us into the space of healing God has for them. If we lead *from* a wound, we will lead many into a pit of despair. This is not God's desire for His beloved. He is always redeeming our lives, if we would only let Him do so. Learn more about this concept in *Leading with a Limp*, by Dan Allendar.

17. **Mind of Christ.** We are called to renew our minds (Romans 12:2), and we have been given the mind of Christ (1 Corinthians 2:16). We are to be together with fellow believers and share our minds, renew our minds, and be of "one mind" (Acts 1:14; 2:24; 15:45; Philippians 1:27). Decisions on Church operation were made with "one mind" and we are to be of this unity in mind with Christ, thinking *with* God, not just *about* Him. 8

18. **Take thoughts captive to the obedience of Christ.** Use the filter of your Salvation helmet. If something you are contemplating letting into your mind, ask "is this something that aligns with God's nature, character or His Word? If not, don't tolerate it, discard it. If you've discovered something you've already let in as a thought, and maybe it's even a belief – confess it, ask God what IS true, and how to move forward in that truth. Whenever you feel anything creeping into your thoughts that are not true, add "And Jesus wants it that way," to the end of the thought. If it doesn't make sense, throw that thought out! You have the mind of Christ!!

Communion

Take communion together by remembering all Jesus did. Read Luke 22:19-20 out loud.

As you now step out into this new season of intentional awareness, and clarity of calling, you can commission One Another into the next chapters the Lord has for each one of you.

Some of you may have a very clear idea of how God wants you to walk this out in this season for His Kingdom purposes. Others of you are still waiting to hear the details from Him. No matter what, you are all designed for God's purpose, and you can now walk this out.

Eph 3: 10-11 states that *through the church the manifold wisdom of God might now be made known to the rulers and authorities in the heavenly places. This was according to the eternal purpose that he has realized in Christ Jesus our Lord,*

The church is supposed to make known to the rulers and authorities in the heavenly places (these are not flesh and blood...these are spirit beings...) the manifold wisdom of God. Go and do that with your life, as created, designed, and destined.

Shalom and Amen

Appendix A

In Christ Verses

To use for continued study on what it means to be "In Christ". For even further study, look up "In Him".

• Acts 24:24

• Romans 3:24; 6:11, 23; 8:1, 2, 39; 9:1; 12:5; 15:17; 16:3, 7, 9, 10

• 1 Corinthians 1:2, 4, 30; 3:1; 4:10, 15, 17; 15:18, 19, 22, 31; 16:24

• 2 Corinthians 1:21; 2:14, 17; 3:14; 5:17, 19; 12:2, 19

• Galatians 1:22; 2:4, 16, 17; 3:14, 26, 28; 5:6

• Ephesians 1:1, 3, 10, 12, 20; 2:6, 7, 10, 13; 3:6, 11, 21; 4:32

• Philippians 1:1, 26; 2:1, 5; 3:3, 9, 14; 4:7, 19, 21

• Colossians 1:2, 4, 24, 28; 2:5

• 1 Thessalonians 2:14; 4:16; 5:18

• 1 Timothy 1:14; 3:13

• 2 Timothy 1:1, 9, 13; 2:1, 10; 3:12, 15

• Philemon 1:8, 20, 23

• 1 Peter 3:16; 5:10, 14

Appendix B

Daily Prayer (Extended Version)

By John Eldredge

My dear Lord Jesus, I come to you now to be restored in you, renewed in you, to receive from you all the grace and mercy I so desperately need this day. I honor you as my Sovereign, and I surrender every aspect and dimension of my life totally and completely to you. I give to you my spirit, soul, and body, my heart, mind, and will. I cover myself with your blood—my spirit, soul, and body, my heart, mind, and will. I ask your Holy Spirit to restore me in you, renew me in you, and lead this time of prayer. In all that I now pray, I stand in absolute agreement with your Spirit and with my intercessors and allies, by your Spirit and by your Spirit alone.

Dearest God, holy and victorious Trinity, you alone are worthy of all my worship, my heart's devotion, all my praise, all my trust, and all the glory of my life. I love you, I worship you, I give myself over to you in my heart's search for life. You alone are Life, and you have become my life. I renounce all other gods, every idol, and I give to you the place in my heart and in my life that you truly deserve. This is all about you, God, and not about me; you are the Hero of this story, and I belong to you. I ask your forgiveness for my every sin. I renounce my sins. I ask you to search me and know me and reveal to me where you are working in my life and grant to me the grace of your healing, deliverance, your holiness, and a deep and true repentance.

Heavenly Father, thank you for loving me and choosing me before you made the world. You are my true Father—my creator, redeemer, sustainer, and the true end of all things, including my life. I love you, I trust you, I worship you. I give myself over to you, Father, to be one with you in everything as Jesus is one with you. Thank you for proving your love by sending Jesus; I receive him and all his life and all his work which you ordained for me. Thank you for including me in

Christ, for forgiving me my sins, for granting me his righteousness, for making me complete in him. Thank you for making me alive with Christ, raising me with him, seating me with him at your right hand, establishing me in his authority, and anointing me with your love, your Spirit, and your kingdom. I receive it with thanks and give it total claim to my spirit, soul, and body, my heart, mind, and will. I bring
the life and work of the Lord Jesus Christ over my life today, over my home, my family, my household, throughout my kingdom and domain.

Jesus, thank you for coming to ransom me with your own life. I love you, I worship you, I give myself over to you to be one with you n all things—spirit, soul, and body, heart, mind, and will. I sincerely receive all the work and triumph in your cross, death, blood, and sacrifice, through which my every sin is atoned for, I am ransomed and delivered from the kingdom of darkness and transferred to your kingdom, my sin nature is removed, my heart is circumcised unto God, and every claim being made against me is disarmed this day. I now take my place in your cross and death, dying with you to sin, to my flesh, to this world, to the evil one and his kingdom. I take up the cross and crucify my flesh with all its pride, arrogance, unbelief, and idolatry [and anything else you are currently struggling with]. I put off the old man. Apply to me all the work in your cross, death, blood, and sacrifice. I receive it with thanks and give it total claim to my spirit, soul, and body, my heart, mind, and will.

I bring the blood and sacrifice of the Lord Jesus Christ over my life today, over my home, my family, my household, my vehicles, finances, over all my kingdom and domain. I bring the cross, death, blood, and sacrifice of Jesus Christ against Satan, against his kingdom, against every foul and unclean spirit, every foul power and black art, against every witch, and against every human being and their spirit, their warfare and household. I bring the cross, death, blood, and sacrifice of the Lord Jesus Christ to the borders of my kingdom and domain, and I stake it there in the name of Jesus Christ.

Jesus, I also sincerely receive you as my Life, and I receive all the work and triumph in your resurrection, through which you have conquered sin, death, judgment, and the evil one. Death has no power over you, nor does any foul thing. And I have been raised with you to a new life, to live your life—dead to sin and alive to God. I take my place now in your resurrection and in your life, and I give my life you to live your life. I am saved by your life. I reign in life through your life. I receive your hope, love, faith, joy, your goodness, trueness, wisdom, power, and strength. Apply to me all the work and triumph in your resurrection; I receive it with thanks and I give it total claim to my spirit, soul, and body, my heart, mind, and will.

I bring the resurrection of the Lord Jesus Christ over my life today, over my home, my family, my household, my vehicles, finances, over all my kingdom and domain. I bring the resurrection and the empty tomb of Jesus Christ against Satan, against his kingdom, against every foul and unclean spirit, every foul power and black art, against every witch, and against every human being and their spirit, their warfare, and household. I bring the resurrection and the empty tomb of the Lord Jesus Christ to the borders of my kingdom and domain, and I stake it there in Jesus' name.

Jesus, I also sincerely receive you as my authority, rule, and dominion, my everlasting victory against Satan and his kingdom, and my ability to bring your Kingdom at all times and in every way. I receive all the work and triumph in your ascension, through which Satan has been judged and cast down, and all authority in heaven and on earth has been given to you. All authority in the heavens and on this earth has been given to you, Jesus, and you are worthy to receive all glory and honor, power and dominion, now and forever. I take my place now in your authority and in your throne, through which I have been raised with you to the right hand of the Father and established in your authority. I give myself to you, to reign with you always. Apply to me all the work and triumph in your authority and your throne; I receive it with thanks, and I give it total claim to my spirit, soul, and body, my heart, mind, and will.

I now bring the authority, rule, and dominion of the Lord Jesus Christ over my life today, over my home, my family, my household, my vehicles, finances, over all my kingdom and domain. I now bring the authority, rule, and dominion of the Lord Jesus Christ and the fullness of the work of Christ against Satan, against his kingdom, against every foul and unclean spirit—every ruler, power, authority, and spiritual force of wickedness, their every weapon, claim, and device. [At this point, I specifically name all foul and unclean spirits that I know have been attacking me, such as fear, doubt, accident, jury, death, the religious spirit, pride, arrogance, etc.] I send all foul and unclean spirits bound to the throne of Christ, together with every back-up and replacement, every weapon, claim, and device—by the authority of the Lord Jesus Christ and in his name. I command the judgment of the Lord Jesus Christ upon the heads of those that refuse o obey, and I send them to judgment, by the authority of the Lord Jesus Christ and in his name.

I now bring the authority, rule, and dominion of the Lord Jesus Christ and the fullness of the work of Christ against every foul power and black art—every hex, vex, and incantation, every spell, weave, web, veil, shroud, charm, and snare; against every ritual, sacrifice, and device; against every vow, dedication, and sacrifice, every word, judgment, and curse—written, spoken, unspoken, or transferred to me. I command them disarmed and broken by the authority of the Lord Jesus Christ and in his name.

I now bring the authority, rule, and dominion of the Lord Jesus Christ and the fullness of the work of Christ against every witch, cult, coven, every channel of black arts to me. I cut them off in the name of the Lord; I send the glory of God to them to turn them in Jesus' name.

I now bring the authority, rule, and dominion of the Lord Jesus Christ and the fullness of the work of Christ between me and every human being—their spirit, soul, body, their sin, warfare, and their household. I bring the full work of Christ between me and [now I name people I've counseled or prayed for, family members, folks in crisis looking to me, etc.]. I command their human spirits bound back to their bodies and their warfare bound to the throne of Christ in their life. I bring the full work of Christ between me and my household and all people, in the authority of Jesus Christ and in his name.

Holy Spirit, thank you for coming. I love you, I worship you, I trust you. I honor you as Lord. I receive all the work and triumph in Pentecost, through which you have come, you have clothed me with power from on high, sealed me in Christ, become my union with the Father and the Son, the Spirit of truth in me, the life of God in me, my counselor, comforter, strength, and guide. I honor you as Lord, and I fully give to you every aspect and dimension of my spirit, soul, and body, my heart, mind, and will—to be filled with you, to walk in step with you in all things. Fill me afresh, Holy Spirit. Restore my union with the Father and the Son. Lead me into all truth, anoint me for all of my life and walk and calling, and lead me deeper into Jesus today. I receive you with thanks, and I give you total claim to my life.

Heavenly Father, thank you for granting to me every spiritual blessing in Christ Jesus. I claim the riches in Christ Jesus over my life today, over my home, my family, my work, over all of my kingdom and
domain. I bring the blood of Christ once more over my spirit, soul, and body, over my heart, mind, and will. I put on the full armor of God: the belt of truth, breastplate of righteousness, shoes of the gospel,
helmet of salvation; I take up the shield of faith and sword of the Spirit, and I choose to be strong in the Lord and in the strength of your might, to pray at all times in the Spirit.

Jesus, thank you for your angels. I summon them in the name of Jesus Christ and instruct them to destroy all that is raised against me, to establish your Kingdom over me, to rebuild the shields and hedges of protection around me and my household, and to minister to me your ministry. I ask you to send forth your Spirit to raise up prayer and intercession for me. I now call forth the kingdom of the Lord Jesus Christ throughout my home, my household, my kingdom, and domain in the authority of the Lord Jesus Christ, giving all glory and honor nd thanks to him. In Jesus' name, amen.

Appendix C

Spiritual Gifts Tests

You may have a test that you prefer and wish to use, but if you are in need of one, I recommend the following resources from LifeWay Christian Resources:

1. Spiritual Gifts Survey (Discovery Tool)

    https://s3.amazonaws.com/bhpub/edoc/DOC-Spiritual-Gifts-Survey.pdf

2. Spiritual Gifts List (List of Gifts and Scripture References)

    https://s3.amazonaws.com/bhpub/edoc/DOC-Spiritual-Gifts-List.pdf

3. Where do you feel God leading you to serve (Discovery Tool)

    https://s3.amazonaws.com/bhpub/edoc/DOC-Where-is-God-leading-you-to-serve.pdf

4. Redemptive Gifts Questionnaire

    https://www.dropbox.com/s/70aql9095yx0051/Redemptive%20Gifts%20Questionnaire.pdf?dl=0

Resources

All Bible verses are from the New American Standard Bible translation. (1995). The Lockman Foundation.

1 The tradition of James Strong; Acknowledging project staff: Robert L. Thomas, Reuben A. Olson, Peter P. Ahn, & Robert G Lambeth of the Lockman Foundation. (2004). *The Strongest NASB Exhaustive Concordance.* Zondervan.

2 https://www.gotquestions.org/Bible-concordance.html

3 Richard Booker. (1981). *The Miracle of the Scarlet Thread.* Destiny Image Publishers.

4 https://www.christianity.com/church/church-history/timeline/1-300/gnosticism-11629621.html

5 http://www.biblebc.com/Roman%20Catholicism/summary_of_trent.htm

6 https://www.healthline.com/health/affects-of-joy

7 W.E. Vine. (1996). *Vine's Complete Expository Dictionary of Old and New Testament Words.* Thomas Nelson Publishers.

8 Jim Wilder. (2020). *Renovated.* NavPress.

Additional Resources

The following is an abbreviated list of a few places to explore more of your own healing journey and the how to live the abundant life God intends. These are some of the resources that I have used throughout my life, as well as from others that I do life with that are helpful and have tools to use in our daily living.

- Promised Land Living
  www.promisedlandliving.com

- Kingdom Living – Jessica Rothmeyer
  https://divine-revelations.teachable.com/p/kingdom-mindset-101

- Wild at Heart – John and Stasi Eldredge
  www.wildatheart.org

- Restoring the Foundations Ministries – You can look up an RTF minister in your area and walk through an Issue Focused Session or a Thorough Format Session. I am a trained RTF minister as well and have experienced the deep healing God has for me, as well as led many others into restoration and healing. You can connect with me here to learn more:
  pamela@blueprintlife.net, www.restoringthefoundations.org

- *Leading with a Limp* by Dan Allendar

- *The Subtle Power of Spiritual Abuse* by David Johnson and Jeff Van Vonderen

- *Life Together* by Dietrich Bonhoeffer

- *Authentic Relationships* and *He Loves Me* by Wayne Jacobsen

- *Grasping God's Word* by J. Scott Duvall and J. Daniel Hayes

Made in the USA
Monee, IL
14 April 2023

31666443R00056